Balboa Press books may be ordered through booksellers or by contacting:

Balboa Press
A Division of Hay House
1663 Liberty Drive
Bloomington, IN 47403
www.balboapress.com.au
1 (877) 407-4847

INTERIOR CREDIT:
ARTWORK & ILLUSTRATIONS: Lynette Papp
CARTOONS: Walter Moore
CHILD'S DRAWING: Gabriel Carlos Pinheiro-Papp

ISBN: 978-1-5043-1737-5 (sc)
ISBN: 978-1-5043-1738-2 (e)

Print information available on the last page.

Balboa Press rev. date: 04/08/2019

BALBOA
PRESS
A DIVISION OF HAY HOUSE

Lynette Papp

Poppa's Present

Text and Illustrations by
Lynette Papp

Dedicated to grandparents and grandchildren

Especially for my grandchildren
Lauren & Alex
Kailah & Ines
Nico & Gabriel
Wolf
Maya & Evelyn-Rose

Preface

This story is based upon my grandchildren's first experience of death of a loved one. The deceased was their grandfather who was affectionately known as Poppa. The main character is Gabriel who was the youngest at the time. Through Gabriel Carlos' eyes, the reader will see how he and the other grandchildren involved themselves in the wake, funeral and aftermath. The story shows the importance of normalising death and allowing children to participate in rituals and open discussion in order to maintain a healthy ongoing relationship with dead loved ones.

The grandchildren's spontaneous reaction to Poppa's death changed the way my family responds to death of a loved one. We are now more open and inclusive. They had the opportunity to be involved, to see the body, create small gifts of art or writing, and keep precious memorabilia from the loved one. These activities, along with small rituals and open discussion of feelings and memories helped the children in the mourning process.

The book is in two parts. The first is a picture book for children with multi-media images representing family members and their voices. In it, the reader will see the importance of memory and stories of the deceased for children. The second part is especially for parents. It discusses grief, how my family managed mourning and a brief description of indigenous New Zealand Maori process.

The story begins with Gabriel's drawing on the night Poppa died...

My name is Gabriel Carlos. I live in a country called New Zealand. I am half New Zealander and half Brazilian.

When Poppa died, I was four years old. His name was Poppa Walter and he was always there.

The day he died, my family were very sad. Everyone cried and told stories about him. I listened while I drew this picture. It is of me burying Poppa. I have a spade in one hand and flowers in the other.

I told everyone at the dinner table that I was burying Poppa. Nobody seemed to listen! Next day, Nana found it and said it was a very special picture. I was glad.

I gave it to Poppa to take with him wherever he was going. Even though mummy did not want us to go into Poppa's room, my brother, cousin and I ran in to see him.

We saw him in his wicker coffin. It was good to see him. He was wearing his cool clothes and brightly coloured shoes. He even had his special Pounamu ring on. Pounamu is the Maori name for greenstone.

People visited and stood around his coffin telling stories about Poppa. They were laughing and crying. I listened. Then I gave my drawing to Poppa to take wherever he was going.

Poppa was very clever and funny. He used to draw cartoons. He did one that looked like someone was sleeping inside a present. I could not see who it was. It was a bit hard for me to understand but looked funny anyway.

Nana was very, very sad. She had lived with Poppa for a long, long time. So long, that it seemed like forever to me.

I told Nana that Poppa was not dead. I said he was not dead because he was still in my head. Because I remembered him, that meant in some way he was alive. Maybe that is what the cartoon means?

Those words made Nana happy. She laughed and said, "That is right, Gabriel! If Poppa is still in your head, then he must be alive."

Nana said memories are a very good way of keeping people alive for us. It makes us feel better to talk about Poppa when we are missing him. Poppa is still alive because I remember him, especially in places we went together. I will tell you some of the things I remember about Poppa.

Every afternoon Poppa had a nap. We liked to tickle him to wake him up. He slept a lot and he laughed a lot too. He had a funny laugh. We had so much fun together.

My brother, Nico and I had many great adventures with him. We had play fights on the sofa, climbed mountains, flew kites, went to the beach, read books, rode our bikes, played ukuleles, and made art.

Poppa would usually read us stories before bed.

Sometimes I would fall asleep before the end.

Mummy said that Poppa would fall asleep too. Then they would carry me to my bed and tuck me in. Maybe Nana would tuck Poppa in too.

Mostly, I stayed awake and had a good laugh with Poppa because some of his books were very funny. I especially liked the one called "Walter the Farting Dog."

Poppa was not like other big people. He made jokes about farting, dog poo, and other stuff like that.

He could make cartoons about almost anything. Often, he drew them at the table. He even drew on paper towels.

One day I was feeling bored, so he made a cartoon for me. It was a joke about the pants he was wearing. Nana had to explain it to me. I did not know they were special pants called Board Shorts for wearing on surf-boards.

Poppa and Nana lived near my house and so do our cousins. We live in a city called Auckland, in a country called New Zealand. Aotearoa is the Maori name for my country. We have other cousins in Australia and Brazil.

We liked to play hide and seek in Nana and Poppa's garden. They had a big old house with a garden that looks like a jungle. There were always heaps of trees to hide in.

Poppa played with all of us grandchildren. He even liked to jump on the trampoline in his garden. It was fun to sit down while he bounced us. We would go up and down all over the place until we shouted, "Stop Poppa!"

He was quite fit for an old guy.

One of the best adventures we had with Poppa was going to a special tree. It is in a park nearby and is all hollow inside.

We called it our Hobbit tree because it looks like a tree from "The Hobbit" movie. It seems magical. My brother Nico and I liked to play in it.

I did not like to go in by myself because it was quite
dark and cold inside.

I would climb in and peek out at Poppa. I wanted him to climb
inside too, so I would not be scared. Sometimes Nico and I would
hide from Poppa and he would pretend not to know where we were.

Poppa always climbed in. We would pretend to be "the baddies" and shoot him with our finger-guns. He would pretend to die.

His big smile would sparkle as the sun shone through the hole in our hollow tree.

Then one day Poppa really died.

Poppa got very, very sick. Nana said he had cancer. Then he died. I learnt that every living thing must die, sometimes even Poppas and our pets.

After Poppa died, Nana took us up to the Stone Valley near our tree. We put all the rocks together to make his name. See how cool it looks! I helped Nico because I was too little to write. It took us a long time and the stones were quite heavy.

Poppa loved stones and collected them. That is why we wanted to write his name in the grass using stones. He also collected many Pounamu pendants because he loved their deep green colour and smooth shiny texture. Poppa usually wore one around his neck and had others hanging on the wall in his bedroom. They are taonga meaning very special in Te Reo, which is the Maori language. Nana let us choose one each to keep in Poppa's memory.

The week after the funeral Nana, Daddy and our aunties took all of us kids up to our Hobbit Tree. Nana put one of Poppa's favourite mats on the grass near the tree. Then we lit some candles and put a photo of him on the mat beside his ashes.

We each had a tiny candle inside a glass and found a place to sit. The big kids sat by themselves. Little kids like me sat with Mummy or Daddy. I tried to think quietly about Poppa and wish him blessings on his journey.

I am wearing my Superman T–shirt and Nezzie is wearing her special hat. We all chose what we wanted to wear. Lauren and Alex wore black. Black is the colour that people wear at funerals. In some countries, my nana would have to wear black for the rest of her life because she is a widow now.

Nico and I carefully chose where we would remember Poppa. It was inside the tree. That is our best memory. Kailah found a special place of her own up the slope a little. Nezzie and Aunty found another big tree nearby.

Now we can visit Poppa at the Hobbit Tree whenever we like.

Nana takes us up there sometimes. We have ice-cream afterwards.

Other times we go with Daddy and Mummy. We love to climb the hill and sometimes we ride our bikes there. The other kids go with their parents too.

The tree in the park is a place to remember Poppa. We think his spirit is there. Many other children go to a cemetery to remember their poppas or family members who have died. They often leave flowers on the grave which has names and dates on it. There are even sometimes photos on the gravestone. But my poppa was cremated, and his ashes were given back to us in a little box after his funeral. We could later choose where to sprinkle them.

I take a Buttercup to our tree for Poppa. It is a small yellow flower that grows wild in the grass. It is nice to take a little present there sometimes.

The tree looks very pretty in the evening, especially when there is a rainbow. It is a good place to remember him. It is nice for Nana to go there when she is sad. It is normal to feel sad when someone dies.

Nana says sadness comes like waves at the beach. Sometimes the waves are big, but they go away and come back another day. Sometimes we do not feel anything for a long time. We are all different, but Nana says it is good to have a cry when sadness comes so we can let the sadness out.

Nana walks to make the sadness go away. Nana walks and walks.
It helps when she misses Poppa too much. One day Nico, Alex and
I decided to try it and go for a big walk with Nana's walking sticks
too. We walked in the park where we used to go with Poppa. It was
fun! We remembered him there too.

We still go for sleepovers at Nana's house, get up early in the morning and have pancakes. We go on big adventures afterwards but now we go with Nana instead. We talk to her about Poppa and the funny things he did, especially when we climb mountains.

Even though Poppa died a long time ago, we remember him when we go for walks to visit Stone Valley and his tree. Not long ago, Nico and I made a cross for him with sticks.

Some people believe that when we die our spirit goes to a special place. That place is called Heaven. I hope that if there is a Heaven, Poppa is there.

At night when Nico and I say our prayers and bless everyone, we bless Poppa in Heaven. Nana believes he has gone into the light.

Poppa brought magic to our world. He was very special. He lives on through all of us kids. We remember him on our special days and celebrations. We remember him when we see his photos, paintings and cartoons. And we remember him when we see our special Pounamu. I like to collect stones even now that I am much older. There is usually one in my pocket. I like to feel their smooth texture.

Now there are three more cousins. Wolf, Maya and Evelyn-Rose who came later. They are our baby cousins. Maybe one day they will read this story.

So long as we remember him, he is still alive. Poppa is not dead. He lives in my head.

As Poppa said in his cartoon – "He's living in the present."

The End

Note to parents

This book is for families with children who have lost someone special. The story is based upon how my grandchildren coped with the death of their cherished Poppa. Although death is normal and inevitable, when it arrives many of us become paralysed when talking about it with the children. This is particularly true in our multi-cultural modern world for families who do not have a religious or cultural tradition to draw upon. Being from one of those families, I created this book to share the story of how my grandchildren radically changed our family's approach to death. "Poppa's Present" tells how they instigated their own involvement in their grandfather's wake and funeral. The result was the lifting of the veil of fear regarding death. Through Poppa's death and the aftermath, they learned that life is a gift and death is a normal part of it.

With a background of diversity - European, Brazilian, Maori, and Chinese roots, the children do not fit any one tradition. Consequently, lack of a homogeneous blueprint can make dealing with death in relation to the children so much more complicated. Hence, the tendency to become somewhat paralysed by it, not involving them and keeping emotions under control.

My family was quite typical of the "paralysed" variety. Thinking we were protecting them, we usually shielded children from the emotional reality so as not to upset them. Open show of grief was rare. Usually for us, when a family member died, the funeral director took over.

A funeral with closed casket would take place after which we would bury the body at a cemetery. It was all over within the week. Occasionally a visit to the grave would occur, but less and less over time. Children would not be involved very much, nor was there open expression of feelings by adults. In my experience, death was scary and hidden as far as possible from the children. I had never seen a dead body until middle life.

This all changed with Poppa Walter's death. After observing my grandchildren hijacking his wake in the most humorous way, I was inspired to create this book. It was the youngest child, Gabriel's process, using drawing and his natural spontaneity, that was the most influential. For this reason, the narrator is Gabriel Carlos.

Whilst the story is true the illustrations are a fictional, multi-media representations of Poppa and the grandchildren. The images reflect the multi-cultural nature of the family, and society in general.

Grief and loss

As a counsellor I am no stranger to working with clients experiencing grief and loss. There are many helpful books and theories outlining various stages of grief such as that of Elisabeth Kubler-Ross. However as anyone who has endured a great loss will tell you, death often catches us by surprise and does not operate neatly in stages as was thought. There is no quick fix. We do not all work through the same stages in adjusting and there is no single process.

Mourning takes time, grief comes in waves and emotions change in no fixed order. Generally, unless grief is complicated, the sadness diminishes over time. Loss usually becomes less painful as our lives grow around it. The memory of the loved one remains while our lives move on.

There are ways that help facilitate the process so that grief heals, we recover, and loss does not become complicated. The cause of complicated grief can be lack of closure, unfinished business with the deceased or traumatic circumstances.

Universally, ritual is one of the ways to assist healing and each country has its own indigenous cultural practices. Religious beliefs and ceremonies can also comfort mourners who are coming to terms with mortality. The ability to show grief openly, talk about it and share it is healthy. This is the reason indigenous cultures often manage mourning so well.

Our indigenous New Zealand culture is Maori. Like many indigenous cultures Maori have a very open and healing ritual for death. It is called a Tangi, and children are usually involved. From the moment of death, the deceased is rarely alone. The body leaves the hospital or home via the morgue to the Marae (Maori ceremonial meeting place). A ritual welcome called a Powhiri occurs and the body lies in state for at least two nights. Open casket is usual and family members take turns remaining with the loved one. Free expression of grief and honest words about the deceased is encouraged. Singing and joking are also appropriate. Prior to a church or Marae funeral service the coffin is closed. Burial is usually on tribal grounds.

After the burial, mourners wash their hands in water and sprinkle it on their heads. The home of the deceased is ritually cleansed with a prayer known as Karakia. The widow or widower is not left alone for several nights.

Our story

Our approach to Poppa's death was influenced by the indigenous practice of open casket. His body spent a brief time at the funeral home where my sister and I washed him. The funeral directors later returned him home where a new family response spontaneously evolved. Poppa lay in an open wicker casket, surrounded by candles and music. Friends and colleagues visited and stood around telling jokes and humorous anecdotes about his life.

Initially the parents of the three sets of grandchildren would not allow the children to see his body. However, one of the families offered their five and eight-year-old girls the choice. Undeterred, the three formerly "protected" grandsons made their own decision and rushed through the house to see the body before their mothers could stop them. I was in the candle-lit room with many friends at the time. We heard the bell on the back-door jingle and little footsteps running down the hall. Knowing their mothers did not want the children to enter the room, I nervously observed what took place. The eight-year-old boys peeped in and one said, "Poppa is looking better. Look, he's wearing his ring and his cool clothes and shoes!" Following their lead, the smaller children spent a great deal of time popping in and out of the room placing drawings and letters in the coffin. What a relief it was for me. There were no nightmares or alarmed, traumatised children. It was all perfectly normal.

My daughter-in-law had been worried about the impact of viewing Poppa's body on her boys. She wisely waited until the next morning to ask them. Nico the eight-year-old said, "It was good, but how come Poppa was wearing his cool clothes and shoes?" His mother explained that Aunty and Nana had washed and dressed Poppa at the funeral home. This caused further confusion for him and he inquired, "How did Nana get Poppa to stand up to dress him when he was already dead?" The practical minds of children never cease to amaze me!

Viewing Poppa's body proved to be natural for the younger children. However, the two eldest girls chose not to view him.

It was good that the children were all eventually able to choose for themselves. It seems that, where appropriate, the earlier the children are involved the easier it is to accept death and heal from the loss.

The funeral was a joyful inclusive celebration of Poppa's life. It took place at a boathouse by the sea with live music and many stories.

His body was cremated.

Days later, the children took part in a ritual memorial with candles at their favourite tree, fondly known as "the Hobbit Tree." Two of the boys, including Gabriel, the main character in the story, made Poppa's name out of rocks in a valley near the tree. The "Hobbit Tree" became the place to visit and remember him from that time onward. The tree, along with Gabriel and Poppa, are central to the story.

Lynette Papp

Printed in the United States
By Bookmasters